Praise for Janelle Ad

The poems in Janelle Adsit's *Unremitting Ent* and spring from the wedge driven between the living and the loved one lost to sudden death. The desire to dissolve the divide, at once futile and incessant, turns each poem into a study of the intimate and unbridgeable space between the I and the irretrievable other. The poems seek wisdom from color, from the objects left behind by and in lieu of the loved one, and from the body—the site of contact and separation—to give the disappearance that is beyond negotiation a form, to make it perceptible and, if possible, comprehensible. A love letter to the dead, this book inhabits the need to memorialize while recognizing the fictions it constructs. A love letter to the living, the book rehearses the efforts of those who remain to fill in the impenetrable absence and to resurrect themselves, however provisionally, from another death, the kind that unbearable grief brings.

CONCHITINA CRUZ,
author of *Dark Hours* and *elsewhere held and lingered*

Grief shatters us, breaks us open, changing us forever from the person we were. When we lose someone we love, the person we were dies too, and we have to forge a new existence for ourselves in order to live in a world without our loved one. *Unremitting Entrance* is about living in that world. In these shattered and shattering poems about the death of her sister, Janelle Adsit grasps at pieces of memory: "I collect these things—chunks, shards, / the wrapped, the waning / hold their incomplete damage . . ." With her broken images and halting narrative, she has written a book of poetry about the kind of grief that almost cannot be expressed, and in doing so she makes a new life from the shards of the past, both for herself and for her lost sibling.

CAROLYN MILLER,
author of *After Cocteau* and *Light, Moving*

Janelle Adsit has written us a weather book, a Colorado-body book, a dead sister book wherein sis and self, can be found anywhere: from the "ear's innermost chamber" to "the sleeves violently indifferent." *Unremitting Entrance* creates pockets: pockets of land ("how durable are the colors of nature"), pockets of psyche ("grief is site-specific") even deific pockets ("there are 63 angels in our parents' house. They are gods of the gaps"). In these pockets is an odd coming of age account—the "promise before a promise could be said." Adsit is showing us how, if we are brave enough to "let it be," even if that let means to allow ourselves to go loose regarding our traumas, the lyric that indelibly holds us into our day to day will refine, will grow us (rather than would a rootless, un-planted lyric). From an initial onslaught of suffering at an irreconcilable loss comes the dynamic of a life lived ("unwrap sight and sound"). What a miracle! "No answers. Only rain, latches, spinning".

J/J HASTAIN, author of *Graphomania*

Unremitting Entrance

Janelle Adsit

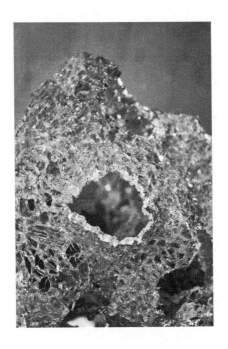

SPUYTEN DUYVIL
New York City

ISBN 978-1-941550-15-1
cover image: Christopher Squier, from *Four Acts of Aggression/ Four Acts against Aggression*, 2014,
shattered automobile glass, thermal adhesives, 30" x 10" x 10"

Library of Congress Cataloging-in-Publication Data

Adsit, Janelle.
  [Poetry. Selections]
  Unremitting entrance / Janelle Adsit.
    pages cm
  ISBN 978-1-941550-15-1
  I. Title.
  PS3601.D755A6 2015
  811'.6--dc23

                    2014023408

UNREMITTING ENTRANCE

Elaborate Struggle

It may be that abstract thinking evolved from our eyes'
elaborate struggle to make sense of what they saw.
—Diane Ackerman, *A Natural History of the Senses*

methodology: the opening is customary
a premise that everything is connected
all oppressions all inches all doors all sky solace
and tree is intersection some are lucky
the window I open to let the if of her in

the opening is customary
but I was not in the room
where the body died there was no room
tissues pressing into one another
flesh folding into flesh
melding as blood expelling
from the body

the opening is customary
under a squally Colorado evening
breath expired blood
letting
out released

car and truck let the one from the other lane in
some are lucky in the folding of metal
onto metal truck that was rushing to a
birth which is flesh extending from flesh
unendingly there are new forms   the baby
into a space of unending new forms   ground sky solace
and tree silent
some are lucky
let the if

View her as inertia. There are laws. She resists acceleration, does
not gravitate toward the outside [the farthest away]. Instead,
the car contacts the passenger, applies a sideways force, so she'll
make [she'll make it] the turn with the car. It is critical to realize
that the force acts upon the car, not the passenger [which must
and did not mean safety].

The gesture of opening the door is foolish.

Mi,

I've been awaiting innate instructions. Listening in on my flesh. I attached myself to my hand. Then I filled my Tuesday like a Big Gulp cup—trying to be glib, frames breaking. Wednesday I wanted you to hand me something and blow the wrapper off the straw, to touch faces with thin, tubular paper.

I want someone to write. Write that I am resisting the aphorism. But you don't write anymore. Your notebooks stacked under your bed, waiting to become memorials. Language enough to be sewn. Put the letters together—a and bri and o and n.

turn this map into sky
turn these 350 blues in the Mountain Bluebird
beating rhythm of blue beating crest
of feather beating skin
turn this rainbow beam of blue, not sky blue
not the second when sky first came into view
the baby arrived blue and wide
this is not the age for awe he says but soon

soon: the tight fist before Amaryllis blossom
soon: photo of her fist in mine
this body maun sune be dust
capture it in gelatin
[there are 176 photographs of my dead sister on display
in the house—the presence of crumbled bones
my father made the film
and called it skin]

sunner suiner soon a definite past and future
schunar in which the time reckoned is indefinite
and the limitlessness of blue

turn this beating rhythm of blue beating
rainbow beam of blue
we could read it her arrival
we could read it blue and wide
an entrance, a song of single come
but this is not the age for awe he says

accelerator and my life is crinkled
into her seventeen years
both of us origami
folding chronologically back
in the search for precedents and parallels:
I want to have seen her death
the precedent is usually in nature

with beauty, the imperative to replicate
I want to find another
but grief is site-specific

I want my creased life to be more vulnerable than this pink
petal curled
petal reminding of its unfurling
petal folded unfolding folding dropping

10. Watch your hands with fingerpaint.

9. Pluck tears and press in wax, something to see.

8. Dress a canvas, knowing how difficult it is to make skin.

7. Paint frost onto a tree branch, cooling those final hands.

6. Build the box for radiance. Leave it open for as long as you can.

5. Weave into the loom of sky.

4. Collage leavings into one.

3. Put a housefly in a model airplane; there are many ways of reaching.

2. Assemble a dollhouse of umbrella. We share shelter in passing.

1. Keep without an object.

there is the swingset we used

to escape

the daycare kids

kicking our feet high above

their heads

I kick

the day

care kids at the funeral chapel

waiting in a line

to see my sister   not there

not here

in this tedious arc not travel

her hand   mine

not holding

———

Durable colors of nature home

———

this phrase cut out of a magazine

our lush discards
this pareidolia

appearing on the floor of my Honda
I want to say out of nowhere

there is no nowhere

there is the depleting green

may observations be imperatives

a car over Overland Trail
a truck in motion on U.S. 287
a crash emblazoned in glassy lights

what we see in it

body and clothes and purse

categorized by amount of blood
withsta(i)n(e)d

how durable are the colors of nature

        my gone sister has been replaced with pink—

the reminiscence of flesh

the reminiscence is the

longest visible
        durable—the face I might see in the forest

of depleting green

        endure: a command for the colors of nature-home

industry can make pinks now that are 99-100% permanent
pink keychain with my sister's face etched into it
pink quartzite bench on a grassy Fort Collins hill,
pink tulips the neighbors planted, pink
candles, pink tattoo of a pink last-gift candle, pink
vases, materials as metaphors—the necessary attempt
at conflation, pink bracelets with her
name—color is more symbolic than sensory
every skin fleck and fingernail
gone to an impalpable gray
in May with its hibiscus pink and its leaving
crabapples, soapwart, begonia

I want to be absorbed
crabapples, soapwart, begonia
absorbing orange, yellow, purple, blue, green

pink a reminiscence of what her skin absorbed
the number of pinks has exponentially increased
how many she is in

I sponge out the pink of her image in the picture
reveal the colors that blot and form her
separating listlessly

the goose   tilts its head up   to swallow
it is tiring to make   in a context of world
she is in the therewhere   the skins can't be accessed
the tree roots excavate the ground

Colorado shower   the hesitation before water hits
the heaviness   behind my eyes resting at the top of my throat
what I do with culminations   her ring on the butterfly-bound board

I have picked at the mattress, trying to enter what she left
the weather presses complex and change
into my skin   her skin
flecks amassed in the cotton and bedsprings
halfway in from the crust   that's how I'll locate it—inaccessibly

her body   anatomized into
ash   like dark salt extracted from skin

she's been gone an accurate number of days
the wind is still coming from the same direction
each breeze over Colorado dryness brings a different color
some sand some salt   some traces   some trace the wind
and its leaving   the dirt on the roots

o sister, were you like a crooked trunk, starting in one place and rolling out of it? the break that crashes metal and metal and inertia and mass and acceleration. the subsequent breaks. we're all colliding. and we turn from it. and you turned. you did not see.

so, sister, farewell with your spreading body. your body that does not hold flesh. that cannot be held. farewell with a slow moving circle. farewell with a silence that I've buried in Colorado red clay. farewell to the pink with which they have tried to vehicle you. farewell with the vases I have ceased to shatter. they sift through.

I am a hook in a river. homestead. take my eyes. hold them.
they will swim. try to fall within. hook me next to her.
press me with—as leaves in wax paper
as bodies between linen and table. we put rivers in bottles.
we cannot be far. only homestead. we grasp at trees.
small fingers into a vast blink.

First seeing:

I know nothing of this place. I walk. it is the labyrinth that
is supposed to help me grieve. dog poop. a black trash can. a
green poop bag dispenser. chimes. the houses that smell like
tea. one bird sounds like a chime's impression of a car starting.
many rust-breasted birds.

Away and seeing:

the rust-breasted birds are black rosy finches. they have no
song. I say they ripple. rallentando. start again. outside my
window, hundreds are perching in crab apple trees, foraging
the dried blood drops. they throw the drops from the branches.
swiftly bound to the ground. then reach the branch again—
their light bodies. the branch gives a little and then springs
back. grandmother told me they damaged her garden. but they
spring back.

melocomerespondedy

I went to the precision of Sarcodon imbricatus
to find the r | h | y | t | h | m of your eyes
on this page. you see only dry print
and your fingers—please ink them, and press.

empiricism: one archaeologist climbs to the cornice
of a Greek temple. another yells: "do you find
any traces of color?"
an affirmative answer. then,
Auguste Rodin striking his chest
"I feel here that they were never colored."

the way we know how to see
is located
in unseen parts

here he can paint the if of her face
here I keep myself in sight

rutted sand and the violent rush of metal

my father calls this place of wind and few barriers

—the intersection of Overland

and U.S. 287—the accident *scene*, not *site*

as if we'll see her leave us

here, be able to collect it

in details, chunks

black shards of car

yellow crumbles of seat foam

a straw wrapper, and the foothills

large only on certain days

cars cleaving air

I collect these things—chunks, shards

the wrapped, the waning

hold their incomplete damage

"let me begin with blindness,"
a boy who helps me grieve
wants me to say   he unlaces my shoes
feels everything—cigarette butts, bird shit
and sidewalk chalk   every wild
within yellow and white lines, sidewalk edges
that feel into the spaces between each ripple

"the reason for living
should not be in the hands
of argument," he mutters against his palm
his fingers spaced against my lips
then he hands me something caught   snapped
as image everything becomes metonymic
her mouth there, not moving not closed not agape

make her lightfast

white: I wear her clothes, wanting their fibers to find my body's fibers

white: Turner left his finished canvases to mold thriving on egg-based primer

red: the taste she died swallowing I try to smell into my mouth

make her lightfast

white: fossilized sea creatures in limestone graves

white: I trace the faded curves and lines of her bedsheets

make her lightfast

red: Turner chose his brightest, knew it would not last

red: press my lips to the dark stain of her wallet

red: women coating their lips in cochineal blood

white: bodies go pop, pop

"it's amazing how empty that was."
at first I think my father is speaking
of her burial ceremony—
how it didn't make a difference,
but he means the box we buried
too large for so little of her
powdered grayness

the small sod rectangle
we added to the ground
so new
to this disturbed earth
planted with my sister
I have only wanted to bear witness
she didn't want to be buried
but there is the need for a place
of emptiness

our place of her
is next to Garcia, behind Smitt
my sister wouldn't sit next to strangers
in church, a mound of our things
on the seat beside her

I contributed to the pile

Second seeing:

I am standing just off the sidewalk. I'm afraid of trampling something. something that will make no sound. I have not learned what can handle the human footprint.

the ripples of the olive-colored water make no sound. in the time I've been standing here, they've moved in four different directions. now I navigate by other than east, west, north, south. by uncertain actions.

there are layers of mud around the lake—each colored ring is distinct. thick mantle, outer and inner crust. the water is the core. this is not symbolism. I am trying only to describe.

a no swimming sign. water's slow progression toward me. collecting symbols, signifiers. we place a sign at the accident site to slow.

Fourth seeing:

something catches my nose in a sneeze. I was impressed yesterday by a poem that included the line: "I blew my nose."

today a woman in a turtleneck walks along the sidewalk— walks all the way around the pond. she does not look at the pond—looks ahead. thick clouds. undefined reflection in the water.

we make the desertion

we remain are remains

we are neither definitive nor infinite

we—the remains preceded us

we into a new distribution

we ash into dew water

we don't dissolve

we into stalk of bluegrass green

we the dew absorbed in color

we make the desertion

we make the Medano Creek desert

we the pores created by sand

we each space between

we vast enclosure

we in the roads and highways

and the glue of blood

we in the somersault of metal

we in speed

we in the empiricism of red and ground

we in the didn't

we into the function of back

we into wanting to continue

longest visible

red: circle, theory of everything
in all three primary color systems
red attracts, appearing in advance
the blood that escaped first
the blood that hit pavement and can't
now be seen   red

seems closer

as it stretches longer
in wave   she was riding to reach the rain

longest visible

she might have stepped out
not noticing how the drops touch
intimately like the whisper's feather-breath in the ear
air touching all of what's inside
the rush into her body
folding unfolding folding dropping

seems closer

less confined now being gone
who knows what constitutes
a life: "The multiplicity of factors
that might collectively
be contributing to its growth
is infinite."

longest visible

each tragedy
claimed to be predictable
surprise
the ability to graph it in hindsight

we might prop ourselves up this way
with philosophical puzzles of (un)knowing

the ash I can't touch
because they've glued
the box shut

I plead: unquantify

I want measurements
an exceeding interest in the remnants
evidence, an accident reconstruction
vectors drawn

diagram the seconds
her eyes open
her seagrass eyes
the pupil wide
among the gray I would know
its decomposition
touch the iris as mossy velvet
suffuse its matted clumps

Do I know the ground that will bring me?
How much do those last seconds hold up?
And how will the sunlight move within them?
Is what vanishes important to your vanishing?
How many sudden days will my life hold?
What color would you have dyed your hair next?
And what of this third conditional—a tense that signifies no possibility?

Mi,

Your suspension of being. I'm painstaking. I've been charting this place, suspended above the dead. Pain and staking. I've been asking the dead if there's room. Noting this cartography of ground and under. The sunlight is a précis. A curved, recursive way of deciding what's prime. I have been repeating steps that won't repeat. And you know that I came into grief without faith and with the weather's oscillation. I believe in wagering and luck and push. But still I need some fixed points. There are 63 angels in our parents' house. They are gods of the gaps.

I'd like to hold things like integers. I counted the angels and the crows flew over a river. Calling here shear bare bare. Yes, rhythm is the cause. The 1 then the 2. This was the promise of our forbearers. Yes they bore deep. The promise in heaping bodies under heaps of dirt. The changed tightnesses. Open through them. And you'll see there is more fraying, more movement that is called death. When they are saying we're better off, get off, fly off the handle. And then you're off. For a while. Then a finish line. And you're surrounded. Call them crows.

—ground-making again

her suddenly not pulsing bare feet   my shoe   not in my hand
the   noiselessness   telling me not to remove it

afterward, I write a treatise on Kleenex
          with numbers,   puzzle pieces, questions
of progress,   a piece of poem   sign it
_____

sign it because we allow this to signify
acceptance-initiation of fact   conclusion
that if the door is yellow   then there is no
light. we must hold fast to the evidence.
sign here: _____
          we lie. we believe. amen.

6pm, weekday, a knock on the door.

most quantities we never know—how many days   this leaf has   seen
the exactness of the volume of ink in the library
the time of death I keep   hidden with her   wallet
the hairs she left   nesting on a brush
12 ounces of a new version of human   weight
signed_____

makeless, please come low. I called you bone ash, then snow. drop
as heads drop. falling to pool. I would have the ground depend
on my feet above. I will bleed the sky-water that's within me.
a cruentation. drop as heads drop. everything is going so well.
makeless, crawl into my throat. water caught in a sky-ground
sphere that I am in. can't trap it, nor you. everything is going so
well. O makeless, find me a flake of snow. the tiny spittle of its
dying on my forehead. you used to leave pools of spit on my skin,
laughing. my skin is what you left.

and when she did not sound
and the motor left singing
the radio still tuned to notes and rests

and when she did not sound
and the motor left singing
she sat at the piano, typed out
a pop song about haunting
that could not address me

and the soundless white pea-coat on the backseat
I rearrange the empty arms
the coat looks brutal
no matter how I position it
I want it to lean into something
I want the fabric in her direction

I leave it—
the sleeves violently
indifferent
as the spacious snow

Let me begin with the creation of space.

This is how we articulate our absence: In two neat rows of airplane seats, we're over Denver, and a fly appears on my fold-down table. Rubbing its thinness together mildly. My companion reveals the folds of the map.

———

Let me begin with the uncertain action.

Outside a restaurant window, he stands hard against the gust of lopsided faces, bees, bags, girls in square-cut shirts. His face closed into sleep. The capacity of a human to die vertically. Of muscles to hold.

———

Let me begin with the apparent.

My companion comes up against me at the window. Looks me in the eye. He vanishes. I'm left with large blueness. How colors appear—transiency. I have not learned the local dialect. Or how to earn the word "we."

———

Let me.

The empty gift wrapping remains in the shape of a book. A vacant shell. I stand at an empty chair. Then at the foot of the bed. This man in large clothes by day is a thin and stretched membrane in sleep.

a horror movie trailer is playing on the ER
waiting room's TV   I expect
there's something that can be generalized from this
perhaps all horrors are fabricated
to some extent   but iambic pentameter is not
the heart's beat
chests don't rise
and fall in a sonnet's time

my breathing weighs more
but I misfeel   the monitor tells
an image of my lungs is my voice-over
narrating me into the regular pace   the ridiculous number
of pop songs about breathing   this great congestion
calling pressure, pressure
stay with it the string of your spine I'm sure
of the ball high above when I'm cool in sheets gathered
my things deliberately the foolish gesture
how our space can hide I ask her will
you alter my sense of body make my skin break
high into a spinning dusky blue? rejoin—

but the term is rarely used in modern discussions

COLORS ARE RARELY

Experiment with how you look at colors in nature;
the colors are rarely like you think they are.
—Simon Jennings, *Artist's Color Manual*

all forms of oppression are interconnected
color asked to perform according to standards
"After all, it is the diversity
and individuality of each material
that painters want to exploit"

color: silence: i|n|v|i|s|i|b|i|l|i|t|y: nonhistory:

can I stare at you, woman, as I stare at the color
of this hibiscus's day-old blossom?

70 percent of the body's sense receptors
cluster in the eyes

is staring the same for you and it? does the damage
does it damage   do you

Local color. n. the actual color of an object with no added effects
of light or shade or reflected color

the actual color = colors

> If I am painting a dark body or a pinkish one, these
> are the colors that appear in my painting, but I will
> add all sorts of other colors, too.
> —Tim Riddihough

what her body
the actual color = colors

Genuine Rose Madder is impossible to match
precisely in hue, strength, and texture
with modern pigments

quantify the colors we've lost
in CMYK and RGB

color of the too-plentiful
Tamarisk is r255, g192, b203

eradicate the imprecision
variance in dipping time,
          speed of travel
brightness of the day,
          the fog that fell low
the place elements were mined
          the crossing point

If I could identify the tinge of my gone sister's shadow
it could be 186 (internationalized, regulated, pantone) or

melocomerespondedy.

All language is a site of loss.
—Rachel Blau DuPlessis, *The Pink Guitar*

five petals, single-flowering tree,
tree is weeping, pendulous,
fruit starts yellow, petals oil themselves,
flowers born in corymbs
the fruit is a globose pome (global poem)
requiring cross-pollination

300 Mongolian words for the colors of horses
an indigo dye is dozens of shades,
each depending on weather
226 words for the color of these bluegrasses
in one—which is many—language
here is the local. no, here.
the cloud's shadow over water
"and today we do not know how to make that
blue," her father said

our words signify those we don't have

...(I)mages obey a kind of moral rule that the sites of strip mines, oil spills, and acid rains will look as awful as national park landscapes look wonderful, and most publications usually further this by casting disaster in small black and white photographs whose compositional standards are not as high.

—Rebecca Solnit, *As Eve Said to the Serpent*

this ink is concept:

C=0, M=0, Y=0, K=100;

no clove, honey, locusts, virgin olives,

powdered pearl, scented musk, jade;

no seal brown, bistre;

no pestle

he discovered the rainbow in a dark room

what was found
inside her frozen body: weighed-down organs
stacked not quite right, organs that should not
have weighed down, not in an age of angelization
not at all when she had lost
blood she was reduced immediately
because that's what it means to mourn
the spider webs of her gauzy fluids
the reds and yellows that were not wiped up
but were absorbed
by the weight of cement or metal or car upholstery

what was found inside her body:
if you freeze the spider web, it will fall to the ground
what was found inside her body: the weight of machinery
and not a god what was found inside her body:
not a choice. not a slow fall. not a loud
what was found inside her body: a snap of metal against cartilage
veins to dust to closed box to red Colorado clay

what was found: an essay by a coroner
that cooed "the dead
don't care." what was found inside her body: an essay of little i's
dotted not in tears or tissues what was found
inside her body after she was on a table
I didn't see
but it was assigned to me

Cumulative seeing:

four strategically placed aspen trees on the other side of the
pond—each look new. one with supporting ropes and stakes.
I am trying to read this without reducing it. call it intimate
and far away. on the west side of the water tamarisk abounds.
introduced to Colorado as ornament, not invasion. in this
world of relocation, all are native at remove. some tamarisk
twigs are blown down.

Fifth seeing:

not every wave line follows the same pattern. what does it
mean that I don't want to know why this is? the gadwalls move
away from me. the water level is much higher today. I don't
know the date. could I recognize the next May 4—this day of
one, among many, dead—by the position of the sun?

again the heaviness at the top of my throat. the weather
makes me feel complex. no, it's not abstract. it's guttural. a
weight that's halfway in from my skin. that's how I'll locate it:
inaccurately. she's been gone 357 days, 22 hours, 13 minutes.
that's inaccurate. the wind is still coming from the same
direction. the water in my eyes does not move. where does this
salt come from? within without—wind blows my pen off the
page. is this collaboration?

the gadwall appears to be bobbing on the surface of the water,
but maybe feels that he is still   a weight in the throat.

Mi,

In time someone fell. The dancing stopped. Nine one one and Kleenex pulled. Off the floor and to a bed. We have long wanted to see each other's beds. The transitions arriving under sheets. We dance. We break to the floor. Nights tumbling into a blast of sunrise pink. The ferocity of beginning anew. Hilarity against his tissue. Tissues folding against flesh. Glasses off and close to the maze of your pores. Find another layer of water under water. Another fall under fall.

—this is the way of it

"too early to say goodnight" is how we said her death

pillowed it   tucked it in

our increasing aversion to the wrecked anatomy

the decline of formal modes of grieving

replaced with a bedtime story of sleep

death is disappearing from our thoughts

as it becomes another concept—a divestment

I feel fine   this and that

the convention of the sandwich arrangement

the way I sang the harmony part

got it right   the way the woman was watching

my funeral lips   the way the concrete hardened

around my sister's still-pulsing handprint

people now have to keep their hands busy

unraveling the facts

POEM SOMEONE

I'm a poem someone else wrote for me.
—Sarah Gambito, "Rapprochement"

there's so little I can give you—
daisies at your stone
and the sound of me
there with you
which is no sound
but it will have to do

the coroner said my sister died   the excessive clarity of it
the coroner said my sister died   we could not see

in the morning they called me to ask for her color
I said pink   they made her amaranth, cerise, thulian
annexing her in Gerbera daisies, ribbons, funeral
table settings, picture frames
they said that she would have liked this
but she is no longer singular
being so many tones and likenesses

in death I want the detailed blue of this hydrangea petal
you won't know it

yesterday we found her blood again
I don't know the longest visible color

we halt when we want our speech to mean more. trying to
dislocate our language. I want to place her behind each thought. to
imbricate her in everything. trap her in brick. yes, I hoard her. her
wilderness, her palpability. I take the things out of her room slowly.
unnoticeably. stuff others wouldn't miss, that she would. hair dryer,
tampons, things not discussed. I edit the landscape-narrative of
her bedroom while my parents hoard the memory of her altruism.
I hoard her indulgence. wayward. when her ashes are spreading,
despite our containers. the flecks of gray body are misting the
ground. is it a gift to leave a piece of the painting blank? the halting
of a brush stroke. the creation of space.

if there were something to do

let what I do be done, put aside
to---------------

July 18 seems to require
the tradition of another loss
daisies wilting
to a stone   pink   burdened
requiring that the ground
feel the absence of your 116 pounds
I don't want to make this day a theme
but keep it as a force
my second-floor apartment is surrounded by vibrant Malus
'strawberry parfait'—no sky or ground, just pink
specks moving together with spaces between

matter is not destroyed
your ashes are boxed still
and clutched—
how to return them?
to what ecosystem do they belong?

in the recurrence of this day

I spread myself to the locatable ground
that was a promise before a promise could be said

I hope my whole life
I keep pasting things into the same notebook I hope

my whole life is a notebook
that keeps pasting the notebook

is a life-hope and the
pasting you say

save the notebook
what you say is a pasting

paste up the save this save that
you save the pasting

isn't it time to admit
the notebook

to admit the whole life notebook
keeps pasting

the slip of paper that says
what was your favorite birthday

a birthday is a life-hope
the notebook is a birthday

the cat dipping its face into the candle
like a cookie in chocolate

the candle is dipping its flame into the face
face into flame   the birthday   the same   notebook

I write in my sister's science notebooks now

school notes, Vitamin K essential for blood clotting
my preface   record what I've heard:

—

right here this morning there was a bird.
it must have fallen out of its nest
or something. it was dying, and I took it
home. it died just as I got home. but it
made it the whole way.

—

look after: record it again: this record

the stem of her breath

a pinecone's opening

a few leaves which hung on all winter

made it the whole way

put together the human heart:
how much time
you'll need:
waves do not move
when you are far enough away

———

show your work:
the music's playing: you know it well enough to give up following it

———

ask the muscle to stay as luck
two steps forward gives one step back

give one step back

Mi,

You've been entered into star charts. Such documents are for finding. I am about to. To see you in a coat of blue feathers, seeming to float around. The way your not-yet-blue lips would touch my wrist. It doesn't mean you live in me.

I would map the remnants of your taste here. I would list the times your fingertips entered air. I would rummage through the wagers behind your steps. You must know that I would be your human balcony. Step into my spine. Leave a track that could be kept alive. The sidewalk gum that marks the clouds as they change at the rate of land. There is never silence when real health is the stilled heart. Your chewing gum changed the pulse. And other wide-ranging things.

—looking for an outgrowth

the ear's innermost chamber is where she resides

I flicked a speck of her ash in there   I hold her high

wanting to live her   I have interrupted an ash cycle

how do I return

her gray speck body? I don't know

the way out of cherry blossoms in May

when she felt final   and calling

from a swingset that circled effortlessly

Where were you going when the wind stopped around me?
Not to you. Not to you.

Where were you going when it stopped me?
To memorialize myself in a caricature.

Where were you going?
I was already there.

How did it come to you?
The new? They told me.

How did it come to you?
The way the iris expands in bloom
    to testify to the possibility.

What was the reason?
Time doesn't stop for the same reason.

wet tissue like skin we're handing to each other
exchanging take care of this for me
weary we are weare

Mi,

He is in the room with me. I feel the time I have—having had
your time in me. We will not enter. Your room empty of the
living until 15 years after. The dust lacing the thin silver frame
of your bedside glasses. He hands things to me. He puts toast
in their slots. I say that you would eat the whole breadloaf.
He makes the bed, lets the light in. Your death is one of mine.
A metonymy. I tell him, "you should get going." I have not
relinquished the you that held of you.

—asserting paper

Mi,

The woman told me that I need to stop going to z. Stay with a, she said. And I wanted to go to sleep. That's when I stop counting. Stop trying to clutch his breaths in my mouth. I let go of his air. He thinks sleep counts as time together, but I can't smell his clutched orchid-hand or the dragon he meets in flight. In sleep, we are separate skins brushing skins. We are movement unclutched. Unmeeting. We are breath into room. In-out-to-of one. Two. Body. Not whose. Transfers of what's held and gone. This is the closest I have to a ghost. You're not amid any of this. Trances and water and elements. We wake to revised air.

—z and a

take on color: flesh pink: the sound of the fingertips of one hand
crashing
against
the other's
palm: T
-bone
and stop

bittersweet: a pink-orange
crayon and an Illinois
yellow why delineate
if next is liquid
or discrete
breathing in and
out of ourselves
who could be and are
next next

injury of translation: "let's hit the sky"   make it hold:

travel a way of imposing order: in the beginning
there was the voyage: she hit the asphalt
but let's call it sky: call today
a date that would bring me some when:
pitch of disintegrating weather:
who can prove
this place: a square has sectioned light for me:

assemblage: hands holding
the corner of a book: handling a lover's breath:
hoping to place home:

I want a different color for everywhere:

as sky sees a monotone quilt of brown: a finite
number of pictures: I ask a moth into my hair:
when it's possible to catch eyelashes:
I want to read her slowly:
my eyes at rest: who can prove

VAIN PAINTING

How vain painting is, exciting admiration by its resemblance
to things of which we do not admire the originals.
—Blaise Pascal, *Pensées,* No. 74.

the art of memorializing:

let it be
don't try to rearrange

let it be
I can still search my fingers
searching for themselves in her hair

let it be
leave no trace

the day after she flew away

                        my sister hated birds

a nest of four bird's eggs surfaced

                        and being unable to speak

from the snarled wreath

                        they said she bent double rainbows

on the front door
of our house of grieving

                        over the funeral chapel and memorial bench

the small being who watched

                        witnessing sunsets best

over the blue-white eggs

                        she unlatched safety

was entirely a heartbeat

                        pins into the skin above my mother's breast

that went away

                        and because I wanted to get away

every time the door opened

                        she sent me car problems

to another broken-eyed comfort

                        (it was her car I was driving

that carried the things of mothering:

                        —lines having been crossed, blurred)

breads, dolls, angels

                        things were appearing everywhere

I wanted to find that bird every time

                        leaving us to wonder

to find the whereabouts of gone

                        what couldn't be sent-said-meant in her
                        meanwhile

but I never could

                        could she come back?

she comes back   no answers. only rain, latches, spinning

eggs blooming into sticky flowers   opened wide

wake to skin absorbing a planet
of rapid colors
all but what Cover Girl calls "505"

in this unfeeling bombardment
I am dwelling in absences:
a nightstand water glass
that no one will water
the way I've learned to look
at leaves so that she is in them

air scattering blue
tossing it as petals
I don't want to have to touch

the ongoing exchange of day
absorbing and releasing absences
swallowing and fleeing them

geese tumbling into trees   from where I sit

this unremitting entrance   I know the world

flecks of snow right through me   so well I can't observe it

saying you are malleable   all time

you are this

sense of the mass of   evergreen

unwrap sight and sound
ask sense to find the small places:

———

crumpled hand of the winter leaf
clutching, clutched

every hand remains

———

sixteen wings' click—
joints and rigid organs
move thin as an eggshell sound

anatomize this deep and supple history

———

search into the touch of two trees
finding a way to braid into one another

fir needles sparse
green cotton in the wind

Seventh seeing:

no black birds moving steadily in the mud. black bird flies in to
the congregation and they scatter soundlessly. they have made
a sound I have missed. mis-seed. I walk in a vast expanse of
moments with her, some as indistinct and bending as blades of
grass on a Colorado plain. one tree I hadn't noticed tangled in the
un-comb-able tamarisk—I am searching for my labyrinth here.

Ninth seeing:

big footprints in the mud today. leave no trace. there is a pink
pebble of chewing gum at the base of one of the tiny aspen
trees. one of the branches is awkwardly bent down. I trace the
wind's touch.

each wave brings a different color to the surface. today,
elsewhere, I heard a tree creak for the first time. it sounded
like a rocking chair. meanwhile, my sister slept dreamlessly.
each day has been equally bright. I have not measured have
seen have noticed have unknown. what traces could be left?

I have left this trace. Trace me.

this evening allows me gray
shades in the yellow-gray of still-sun sky

"perhaps the night is even more
colorful than the day"
perhaps the gray

the myrtle green branch
searching into the parking lot

———

this pile of words:
swirl of distant roadway

———

february's ice the texture of her rumpled skin
evening light lull
  that ran along her voice that day

—

how has my
outlandish
unease found place on land?

stance open as cleared land
rows of mounded mud word the vast ground

feel the tiny holes where seeds once made room—
you are among them

---

you tried the rock's odd posture
sloped against it
turned as a hand around a cup
you shape yourself to the feel of things
and they come through

---

your body limp and discarded
littered on the sand
an arm of a tree tries you
hesitant to check for your life

does this dirt
of gold, white, berry,
and assurance
become tedium for the geese swirling
above in the snow-stained winds?

why have I thought that places repeat?
as we pass green squares from 30,000 feet

Prairie Cascade Willow, European Larch
French Pine Pussy Willow
Privet's small black beads know
a flying bead in the sky

they have thrown their branches
down on the path where I am
careful not to step
not knowing what the thin
parts
reassemble

dragonfly lay
her flight down
to concrete
made the definite cold
as safe as amber

I'm the place she let me

together we might make an
entire touch

Mi,

You're gone. And I don't think it matters whose world pulled out. I'm trying not to think of us—or anything—as different. Forever has a way of sweeping everything together: flesh, a laugh, your scream. Now winter will come and go at once/ as constant/as Christmas/as light-up palm trees with strings of glowing grapes pretending to pulse round and round. We try to make it more than what it is. We use words like parlor, home, chapel...   could as well be nectar. On Thursday, you were descending the staircase, bouncing and chewing gum loudly. You were on your way out. Now you float, never chew, are always home. Of course home is a place you've never been, where you know hardly anyone and can't call out. But you have no pain, no matters. I'm thinking of the circuit breaker. And breaking. Breaking in. To paint by numbers with you. I know the spaces are small, but we'd fill them.

—

Dedication

now between us there is only
the space between an ice cube
and a bubble which is which
pen we will take in which hand
of our hands whose hand in our hand
we don't write to each other
having reached a distance   hard to carry through

if I name the color of this spot
on the crabapple   pahlomay
that's what it sounds like
(not pink noise, density not being proportional to frequency)
could it accurately describe the tinge of heart
of a dying man one floor above?

the last place
will know itself only as soon

soon.

may this make it to you

Unnamed sources include: H.B. Marriott-Watson's "The Dying of Death," published in *The Fortnightly Review*, issue 72 (August 1899); Nicholas Harberd's *Seed to Seed*; and Victoria Finlay's *Color: A Natural History of the Palette*.

Angelization is a word used by Marshall McLuhan.

Acknowledgments

I am grateful to the editors of *Better: Culture and Lit, Caketrain, Crucible, Inkwell, Oyez Review*, and *Red Clay Review* who first published several of these poems (sometimes in slightly different forms). Appreciation also to Matthew Cooperman and Veronica Patterson for their thoughtful responses. And to Tod Thilleman and Nava Renek at Spuyten Duyvil for taking care in the publication of this book.

This book is dedicated to Kayla.

And, always, love and gratitude to Shawn. Ring ring ring ring.

JANELLE ADSIT's poetry, essays, and reviews have appeared in journals such as *Sixth Finch*, *Caketrain*, *Mid-American Review*, and *Colorado Review*. She received a PhD in English from SUNY Albany and is currently a postdoctoral fellow at Simon Fraser University in Vancouver, British Columbia.

Made in the USA
Charleston, SC
08 September 2015